Breath

Also by Prem Rawat

Hear Yourself

Peace Is Possible

Breath

WAKE UP TO LIFE

Prem Rawat

ST. MARTIN'S
ESSENTIALS
NEW YORK

First published in the United States by St. Martin's Essentials,
an imprint of St. Martin's Publishing Group

www.stmartins.com

Illustrations and endpaper art by Prem Rawat

The Library of Congress Cataloging-in-Publication Data is available upon request.

ISBN 978-1-250-36675-7 (hardcover)
ISBN 978-1-250-36676-4 (ebook)

Our books may be purchased in bulk for promotional, educational, or business use.
Please contact your local bookseller or the Macmillan Corporate and Premium Sales
Department at 1-800-221-7945, extension 5442, or
by email at MacmillanSpecialMarkets@macmillan.com.

Originally published in Japan by Bunya Publication in 2022

First published in the United States by St. Martin's Essentials

First U.S. Edition: 2025

10   9   8   7   6   5   4   3   2   1

In memory of David Passes,

who helped inspire this book

Contents

CONTENTS

Preface

It has been said many times that a journey of a thousand miles begins with the first step. The same is true in our lives: every journey of a human being begins with that first breath.

We will breathe many times, and ultimately, there will be the last breath that will see us cease to be in this world. But a life is not just defined by all the things that we do, but by everything that we learn and gather in our heart.

How important is it to understand that the breath is truly a gift? It is incredibly important, because believe me, we take this breath for granted. Yet this is one thing that we cannot allow ourselves to do. We need to see its beauty.

We need to admire what this is all about. In the midst of circumstances beyond our control, there is a reality that we exist, and this existence is made possible by the courtesy of this breath, coming in and out.

Many people have tried to understand what that means, but you have to experience what life is. You cannot just give life a meaning, an arbitrary meaning; you have to experience what it is.

What does it feel like to be alive every single day? To be at the cusp of this existence where in one sense everything around us is trying to destroy us. On the other hand, this breath that stands with us is making this most beautiful thing called existence possible.

We are, and it is inevitable that one day we will be gone.
The distance between the two walls, the wall that we
came through and the wall that we are going to go
through, defines what we are all about.

You could be anyone. You could have been anyone,
and you may have a big possibility to be anything and
anyone you want to be, but you can never forget that all
this will happen because of the courtesy of this breath.

This book, in its beautiful way, tries to bring forth the
reminder and the understanding that is unique to what
this breath is all about. And really, in a way, it is pointing
towards our own existence. You, me, being alive.

Because we are alive, there is a plethora of possibilities that open up. Some are good, some are bad, but the possibilities open up. It is up to us what we decide to accept, either those possibilities in our lives that are good, and to move forward with those, or to make mistakes and never learn from them. That is also a possibility, but it is not a pleasant one.

Awakening to this incredible miracle called life is the most wonderful thing that we can do.

I sincerely hope this book brings and awakens a message in you, in your heart, and that you learn something that is very, very precious, something that has been mirrored for time immemorial, through the ages, by so many before us, and most likely will still be echoed by so many after us.

While you're alive, this is a unique opportunity.

Thank you.

Prem Rawat
June 7, 2022

A breath comes in and a breath goes out and you find yourself alive. The palette of what you can feel is virtually infinite. This is the realm of the heart.

Introduction

So many writers of the past have described how important breath is, how fundamental it is to the life of a human being. They have characterized breath as a gift. But are their words understood today?

Breath is a gift that we share with every human being on the face of this earth. We may have different opinions, different ideas. We may wear different clothes, do different things, have different cultures. But we all take a breath. Breath is the beginning of life, the sustaining of life, and when it ceases, it is also the end of life.

Breath is a silent message to each of us: "Wake up. Wake up to life!" So far you have only woken up to your world, to your responsibilities, to your dreams.

But you haven't woken up to life. That is a whole other step. And when you wake up to life, you understand who you are. You understand who others are and that they are not any different from you.

Then you understand what peace is and the value of peace in your life.

I.
What Is Breath?

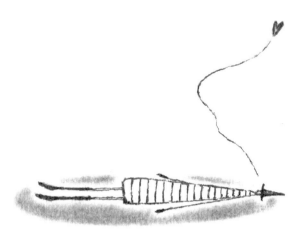

1 First and Last

When you came out of your mother's womb, the discussion wasn't about whether you were a boy or a girl. You know what the question was in that first moment? "Is it breathing?"

Everybody in the room holds their breath, literally, as the physical body comes out—blue, slimy, not very pretty—until they hear that baby's first breath: "Waaa, waaa!"

But do you know how the first one began? In! Not out. There was nothing to go out. The first intake of breath. And then everybody gives a big sigh of relief.

Immediately after that first breath, the baby goes from blue to pink. Now the baby is alive.

Fast-forward to the end. Again, there is the body. Everybody is very still, very quiet. What are they waiting for? The last breath, which finishes with going out. And not coming in again.

This is how it is. And if you are hooked up to a monitor in the hospital and it goes, "Beep, you're dead," yet you are still breathing, who do you think the doctor will hit? You or the monitor?

The doctor will not hit you and say, "You stupid idiot, you're dead! See, the monitor says so!"

No, the doctor will hit the monitor! "You stupid monitor, you're lying! You're broken! Because this person is still breathing."

Your breathing is your life certificate.

What is real? It is the breath that comes into you. It is your existence.

The day you took your first breath, all possibilities of failure stopped. You were a success. As long as the breath keeps coming into you, you are successful. And that breath that just came? Success! Don't you understand? Being alive is success!

Your breath comes freely, bringing the gift of life. And it leaves so that it can come again. This little motion goes on and on. In perfect stillness, there is this motion. No judgment. Every day, every night. That's your entire universe. Within the realm of that coming of the breath and going of the breath is your entire universe.

Because one day, the breath will go out and it will not return. Kind of funny, isn't it? Goes out. And that's the last one. It does not return. The coming doesn't happen anymore. Your universe, that second, ceases to exist.

Defying death, to a lot of people, is thrilling. Actually, every time you breathe, you defy death. No need to go bungee jumping. Bungee jumping happens every time breath comes into me. See the power of breath?

Somebody sent me a letter—a terrible situation happened to them and they mentioned in one line that they no longer saw a purpose for them being here. My view is that you may not see a purpose, but rest assured that if the breath is coming into you, you have a purpose. Now, you may not see it. It may not be apparent or obvious to you. But if breath is coming into you, you do have a purpose. If, after hearing this, you embark on a journey of discovering that purpose, then wonderful. If life seems aimless to you, then look at your breath.

Death is powerful. It spares no one. Not even the planets. Not even the suns or solar systems. Not even the galaxies. Do you know the only thing that's keeping death away from you is your breath? How powerful is that? Do you have any idea? How delicate is that?

What is the power of it? It's keeping death at bay! So long as this is happening, death cannot come. And when this stops, it doesn't matter what you have accomplished in your life, how much money you have, how many friends you have, how many powerful people you know, how muscular you are.

We do not pay attention to the breath. We do not see it as a major factor in our existence till the day it starts to leave, and then it becomes everything.

You could have everything that you want—and more!
And yet, if this breath—which is air, by the way, just
this stuff that's everywhere—doesn't come into you, you
are finished. No more anything! Nothing!

If your ice cream falls to the ground, don't worry, you can get another one. But all the wealth in the world cannot buy you another breath.

The time you think you have is an illusion. Before you're even able to gather yourself, it's time to go.

Your life safety net is made out of breath. When even your power to speak goes away, breath is the only thing that will still rumble through you, and it will be the last thing you know as it fades away.

A little air comes into you, brings you something, then goes, brings you something, then goes, again and again and again. How did your life begin? With the first breath coming in. How will your life end? With the last breath going out. And in between it coming in and going out, there's a story.

Somebody got lost in the middle of the ocean—there's a story. Somebody got lost in the middle of the desert— there's a story. Somebody was really rich but then lost everything—there's a story. The homeless person won the lottery—there's a story.

But the story of stories is the one between the breath that came in and the breath that went out. There's an amazing story—and it's your story. It's the only story that you know is your story. And it's going to keep on unfolding till that last breath.

Because you are alive, you are the recipient of this breath. If that breath stopped, you would no longer be alive. You would be treated just like this: "Whhhsht! Out!" Out of your own home.

There are people who say, "Oh, nobody can take me away from my home! This is my house! This is my home! And I get to defend it!" You have heard those people, right? Well, when this breath is gone: "Whhhsht! Out!"

So, what's going on here? It seems to me, the whole world is saying, "Me, me. I am. I am this, I am that." But without the breath, there's nothing. There is no understanding of the breath. There is no understanding of what it means to be alive.

What Is the Most Important Part?

Once all the parts of the body had an argument about who had the most important function to perform. "I am better than you. I am greater than you," each proclaimed. So they decided to leave the body one at a time and see how long it could survive. So the hands went, then the legs, then the arms, and they all came back and asked how the body had survived without them. It said, "Not too bad. Not too bad at all."

But when the time came for the breath to leave, all the other parts felt themselves losing their power and their consciousness, and they screamed out, "No, please don't leave! If you leave we will certainly be dead. We now understand. The breath is definitely the most powerful part of the body."

So what is this breath? What is this power without which no human actions can be performed? This is the thing that you should know and that I would like you to know.

All the doctor has to say is, "You have only two months to live." That's all the doctor has to say and enlightenment begins: "Oh my God!"

Understand that right now something is keeping you alive. You don't need to know its name. There's something that is keeping you alive, and that which keeps you alive is doing you a favor. It is giving you a gift.

When the bad day comes, you will know the value of breath. You will. But you won't be able to do anything with your newfound wisdom. And I want you to understand the value of breath now, while you're still alive and can enjoy that wisdom.

We have schools, universities, and training. How to learn languages, how to speak, how to write, how to do math. But there is no education in this world about how to be you. Nobody teaches you that.

All your life you have tried to win the respect of other people. You did whatever you did for other people. You don't live life for yourself, but for somebody else.

Who does this breath come into? You! It comes into you! Can you give a minute of your life to somebody else? If people could sell five minutes of their life, do you think there would be anyone poor in this world? Rich people would pay a lot of money for that! But you can't! You cannot give even one minute of your life. So who are you living this life for? Life is living itself for you.

What have you been given? It began the day you took your first breath. You were given an opportunity to be, to exist. You have the possibility of truly being alive.

Your life began when you started breathing and will end when you stop breathing. It is the beginning note and the end note of your symphony.

What do you have in the middle? Nothing, if you have not learned the value of this breath. This is everything you are. This breath is taking place—without any effort. Feel its motion. It is happening automatically.

It is a blessing that this breath comes into me—unasked for. No button to push. No phone call to make.

One breath at a time. It has nothing to do with the past, and it has nothing to do with the future. It is only in the moment called now that you actually exist. You cannot exist in the future or in the past. Future is your wishes, past is your memory. The moment called now is sheer magic.

When we accept the importance of the coming and going of this breath, our lives will transform.

The Divine sign is literally under your very nose. So long as this breath comes into you, you have the power to do what you need to do. That is your sign!

2   Exclusively for You

From the workings of the universe, something stirred
and this breath came exclusively for you.

You live. You exist. You can think. You can see. You can
admire. You can touch. You can feel. You can analyze.
You can laugh. You can cry. You can be a dad. You can
be a mom. You can be a brother. You can be a sister.

You can be whatever you are. Courtesy of breath.

Approach the topic of this breath as the day approaches
you. The sun begins to rise, gently, gently, gently. And in
the evening, simply, without any fanfare, it sets. You fall

asleep and rest, to awaken again in the morning. This is how simple it is. This is what is going on around you.

The most powerful thing in your life, breath, unannounced, comes into you and it fills you. And life is breathing. It comes and it goes. It has a rhythm and simplicity. You don't have to do anything. It comes and it goes.

The song of life is played on an instrument called breath. Look at this life. Look at this existence. The breath comes—no judgment, no prerequisites, no forms to fill out, no lines to stand in, no waiting game, no dot net or dot com to log onto. It just comes. Life dances and plays out every day in the most serene and simplest of ways possible.

You weren't made with a cookie cutter. All these people have been created, yet no two are alike. Not even twins.

That is so personal—to craft every single being with so much care. Every day to have that breath come—that is an amazing amount of detail.

Your life is not about seconds, minutes, and hours but about every breath you take.

Trying to find beauty that satisfies, people look at forests, deserts, mountains, oceans. Yet how many say, "Look at this breath. How beautiful this is!" Look at this existence and see how beautiful this is.

This breath comes and touches me like a harp. It plucks that string, and an incredible resonance vibrates through my whole being.

This body is dirt, pure dirt. New, old, beautiful, ugly—
dirt all the same. But right now, on this little patch, it's
raining. It's raining breath.

You know what is really new? The breath that just
came. That's the newest thing in this whole universe.
You just got it. And it left. And here comes a new one.
And it just left. And here comes another one. I'm trying
to point out the magic of that existence to you. Just the
magic that's there.

So moving yet so still, so obvious yet so transparent,
so complex yet so simple, so sure yet so uncertain, so
precious yet so free, so numerous yet one at a time,
breath comes.

The same power that drives the universe breathes us.

We have been chosen to be the platform for life.

II.
The Importance of Breath

1 A Valuable Gift

You, me, everybody in this world, we judge ourselves. "How am I? What degree do I have? How big is my house? How many cars do I have? How many clothes do I have? How many rings do I have? How much do I have in my bank account?"

We see somebody else, and we say, "I wish I was like that. That's what I want."

But can you judge yourself with a different scale? It's called the "scale of life." Then you will see that the most magnificent of gifts comes to you: the gift of breath.

Even if you live to be a hundred years old, that's only 36,500 days. It's not very much! How important it is that every day needs to be in contentment! Understand the value of every breath that comes into you.

Breath is necessary, so it has been removed from your supervision. Otherwise, it would be like the next story.

Don't Remove My Headphones

A lady goes to a hairdresser and says, "I'd like a haircut—but there is one condition. You can cut my hair, but I don't want you to remove my headphones." The guy is very curious. But he says, "No problem," and gives her the haircut.

A few weeks later she comes back with the same request. "I'd like a haircut," she says, "but don't remove my headphones."

By this time, the hairdresser is really curious. "What is she listening to?" he wonders. So, while she's sitting in the chair, he removes the headphones.

To his great surprise, the woman keels over and dies. He's shocked.

The ambulance arrives and the body is taken away. The hairdresser is stunned. "What was she listening to?" He picks up the headphones, puts them on, and what does he hear? "Breathe in, breathe out, breathe in, breathe out. . . ."

There is a clock on the outside and there's a clock on the inside. The clock on the outside keeps getting faster and faster and faster and faster. What about the clock on the inside? Its pendulum, its swing is every breath that you take. It doesn't speed up. It's there. It's beautiful. It's kind.

Can you imagine if every time we had to take a breath, we had to push a button? It would drive us crazy. Because that's what we would most likely forget to do.

But, no! Without asking, without putting a coin into a machine, breath comes, bringing with it the most magnificent gift of life, the most magnificent gift of existence.

Is this a gift? I call it a gift. It doesn't matter what I call it. Do you think it's a gift?

Breath comes and each breath brings the possibility of being fulfilled.

What you are looking for is within you! Always has been and always will be.

The story is not very complicated. It's very simple. If the Divine is everywhere, then it's within me, too.

Human beings forget what it means to have this breath. We pray for so many things. But who prays for a breath? "One more . . . ."

That which is most precious to you is given most abundantly. But because it is given to you most abundantly, that does not mean its value is any less. It still remains the most valuable.

Of all the relationships you have, do you have a relationship with this breath? Do you understand it? Do you know it?

I'm trying to remind you of what you know. Sometimes that's what clarity is. Sometimes clarity is to be reminded of who you are. To understand the preciousness of this breath, to feel alive every single day.

"The coming and going of this breath is a blessing."
When I first heard that, I thought, "Yes, of course." But
this comes as a surprise to many people. They know
it and yet they ask, "God, if you are there, give me a
sign!"

What sign do you need? Here is the sign. Right under
your nose is the sign. But people don't see it. They want
a rainbow, they want lightning, and God gives a breath.
"Agh! How can breath be it?" What? Too simple for
you?

So, did the breath just come into you? It did. Do
billionaires breathe? Do the poor breathe? And oh, by
the way, how much do you think a breath costs?

There isn't enough gold, enough diamonds, enough money on this earth to buy one breath! And it just came into you! Again. And again. Coming, coming, free!

You are so rich! Understand how fortunate you are. The priceless is coming into you. You are being touched by the priceless every single day.

There's something happening in your life that is more important than the sum of all your accomplishments and your mistakes put together.

What is it? It is the coming and going of each breath.

Could it be that the miracle of all miracles is the coming and going of this breath? Could it be that I have been living on top of a gold mine every single day?

Every breath holds the key to your happiness.

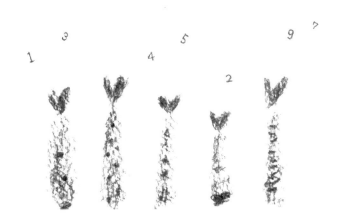

2   Finite and Infinite

Within, you can feel the endless moment—out of nowhere, into somewhere, and then out again into nowhere, one breath at a time.

Is breath really timeless? To answer this, you have to understand what breath represents to us. What does it mean?

Breath comes into you and you are alive. Breath represents not just an exchange of oxygen and carbon dioxide. It actually represents life—existence.

This breath is the manifestation of life for you. The power that ripples through the whole universe comes through you in the form of the breath, and makes it possible for you to be. To be, so that you can understand.

Only then, and then alone, does this breath become timeless—because your understanding is timeless.

Then you have exchanged the finite for the infinite. You have become the ultimate alchemist. You have taken earth, you have taken dust, and truly converted it to the priceless. You have taken something that is so common and converted it into something that is uncommon.

You have understood that being here is not only about the passage of time. But you have reached out of this and dared to touch the timeless. The finite, which you are, has dared to reach for the infinite. And that's when this breath becomes timeless. That's when this existence becomes timeless.

One breath in and one breath out. Can't take two breaths at the same time. Without doing anything, whether you're sleeping, whether you're awake. Within this world of infinite changes, something has been placed that doesn't change inside of you.

A breath doesn't appear to be much. But look a little bit more, and you will find an existence. Look a little bit more, and in that existence you will find the thirst to be fulfilled. Then look a little bit more, and you will find the infinite well of that water that the thirst exists for. And when you can drink that water, you will be fulfilled.

A person is just dirt, but what has decided to come and reside in this dirt?

Turn within, feel this breath. This is the most incredible miracle there is!

Dirt can dance! Dirt can speak! Very unnatural.

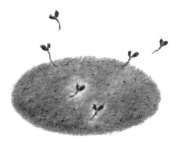

But done with so much charm and grace, it is completely natural that dirt can speak, dirt can think, and dirt can feel the ultimate.

The source of the joy that you want, that will always be there, is inside of you, not outside. I have a heart, and to ignore my heart is the most illogical thing on the face of this earth. How can I not understand that water will quench my thirst? But where is the pleasure the water brings? Is it in the water or is it in me? The sweetness of the mango is in the mango, but enjoying that mango is inside of you. Quenching the thirst, this is the possibility. This is the strength of the water, but the pleasure of having the thirst quenched is inside of you. The one that you are looking for is inside of you. The holiest place in the whole universe is inside of you.

It is my pleasure to remind you what a beautiful, incredible gift you have: this life, this breath. Enjoy! Because that's the only thing you don't have a limit for! Get as much as you can, and then some more!

There's no other reality as real as the reality of being alive. You can feel it. This is as "feeling" as it gets! Now just plug in this incredible feeling machine to the ultimate feeling, and you've got it made.

How lucky for all of us that the ultimate feeling is inside of us. We don't even have to search.

Imagine the timeless, the infinite. Here. And you get to join it. In that moment this breath becomes timeless.

Realize that there is a sweet reality so far away from all the things that you see in front of you. There is a beautiful reality so different from all the good and bad that is happening.

Good / Bad

There was a man who one day lost his horse. So he went to a wise man and said, "My horse ran away."

The wise man asked, "Do you think that's bad?"

The man replied, "Yeah, it's terrible! I loved that horse."

The wise man said, "Okay. Maybe something good will happen."

A few weeks later the horse returned with another horse. So the man went back to the wise man and said, "Oh, thank you for your advice. Something good did happen."

The wise man said, "Do you think that is good?"

And the man replied, "Oh, yeah, I think that's really good, because the horse returned with another horse. Now I have two beautiful horses."

The wise man said, "Well, maybe something bad will happen."

Soon after, the man's son was riding the new horse, and he fell off and broke his leg very badly. The man returned to the wise man and said, "You were right. Something bad happened. My son fell down and broke his leg."

The wise man asked, "Do you think that's bad?"

The man replied, "Oh, I think that's terrible."

The wise man said, "Well, maybe something good will happen."

A war broke out, and the king asked for all the young men to be conscripted into the army to fight. But because the man's son had a broken leg, he was not conscripted.

Everything changes. If you think things are good,
wait a while. It will all change. If you think things are
bad, wait a while. It will all change. You change. The
mind changes. Thoughts change. Ideas change. The
world changes. Everything changes, changes, changes.

One thing does not change: the coming and going of
this breath. It comes and it goes, it comes and it goes.
And when it changes, then all the changes stop. For you,
all the changes stop.

Find your friend within. Find your comfort in this
blessing. Find your joy in this reality. Find your shelter
in this beautiful place. Feel that joy. Feel that beauty. It's
for you, so you can be content.

There are times when problems become so insurmountable that all the strength you thought you had vanishes. The waves get huge. The boat is small. What do you do? It is not a joyride. If you go forward or back, the waves are the same.

Where is the boat of your life anchored? What precautions have you taken? That's the question. The size of the waves is not under your control, but taking precautions is under your control. When you have found a way to anchor yourself in that ocean, in this breath, then you have taken proper and correct precautions. In this breath you find your home. In this breath, you find your anchor. In this breath, you find your reality.

Will storms come in your life? Yes. Absolutely. Will
confusion knock at your door? Absolutely. Will you
be in dramatic situations that are out of your control?
Absolutely.

But just remember that even when the wildest storm
engulfs you, when chaos is afoot, when the night is as
dark as it gets, there is still a lamp that is lit within you.
Even when all seems to be as bad as it gets—and I will
not underestimate how bad it can be. As long as this
breath is coming in and out of you, you still have the
companionship of the divine. When storms make you
feel weak, know that the greatest strength lies within
you.

Be thankful for each breath. Tie your boat to the timeless. Your boat will be secure. If you tie your boat to the changeable, the boat will be smashed. When the heart is full, it's a wonderful life. To the heart, a day got saved, a lifetime mended.

Your potential is the potential of understanding. Understand the timeless. Understand this life. Understand the joy. Understand what it is to be human. And every day awaken to the possibility of your heart being full.

Know how to relate to that perfection that dances inside of you. That is when you begin to understand the timeless breath.

One moment would be enough. You have been given a lifetime to experience it—to know it, to see it, to enjoy it, to feel it.

As long as this breath is coming into you, you are being kissed by the infinite.

3   Know Yourself

The simplest thing on the face of this earth is your breath coming in and out. Stand outside and watch the sunrise or sunset. Observe the beauty, the power of this entire universe in action, this earth spinning with you on it, with this breath going in and out of you, with a heart in you wanting to be fulfilled. These are the simplest of things.

It doesn't need glorification. This story of the human being just simply needs to be told.

There is a challenge and an adventure every day. It's an adventure of understanding. Not climbing mountains. The biggest mountain you will ever climb in your life is the mountain of understanding.

Once you climb that mountain, you truly conquer because you understand. Understand who? Understand the self.

Every day that this breath comes into you is a perfect day. When every day being given to you is perfect, who makes your day imperfect? You are the person holding the scales and bending them, twisting them.

What are you? On one hand, ninety-nine percent of you is oxygen, hydrogen, calcium, carbon, nitrogen, and phosphorus. That's it! Every day you shed ten billion flakes of dead skin. In a year, that equals five pounds of dead skin.

Who are you? You are the perfect instrument, and when this instrument is in tune, it can produce the truest and most beautiful tones.

So far in your life, you have only allowed your mind to play the instrument that is you. Once in a while, you hear a twang, and it seems to be a pleasant note, but so far, no good symphony has been produced.

Be in tune with the reality inside of you. Then you will hear what this instrument is capable of. When you are fulfilled, the passion, the joy, the contentment that comes out of this instrument is unique.

Look in the mirror of the heart and you will see your true face. You will begin to see what a miracle you are. That you've been created by kindness. That you exist by kindness. That the gift of breath is given to you by kindness.

If you don't see your heart, if you don't see the divine in you, if you don't see your strength, if you don't see the blessing that this breath is, that is because you are so far away. So far away, you can't see it. Come closer. Come closer to yourself.

There is a heart. There is a recognition. There is an understanding. There is a value. There is a feeling. There is a thirst. A lot of people say, "I don't feel the thirst." If you don't feel the thirst, it's because you're so far away. Come closer to yourself. If you don't feel that you want to be fulfilled in this life, then that is because you are so far away. Come closer to yourself. The closer you come, the clearer it will become to you.

True excellence starts when a person falls in love with this life, with their existence.

Concepts are the chains that tie you down. They prevent you from seeing the beautiful reality of everything. The beautiful reality of the breath.

Lord of the Jungle

One day there was a rabbit going along in the jungle when a huge lion jumped out. Huge! The lion said, "I'm going to eat you."

And the rabbit thought to himself, "I am finished! I better think quickly." So the rabbit said to the lion, "No! You cannot eat me."

The lion looked at the rabbit, and said, "Hey! You are just a little rabbit. My teeth are bigger than yours. What do you mean, I can't eat you? Of course I can eat you."

The rabbit replied, "No, you cannot eat me because I am the lord of the jungle."

The lion roared, "No, you are not the lord of the jungle. I am the lord of the jungle."

"No, I am the lord of the jungle," the rabbit replied. "And I can prove it."

The lion said, "Okay, prove it!"

The rabbit said, "Follow me and you will see how all the animals in the jungle are afraid of me."

So, if you can imagine, there was a little rabbit and behind him is the big lion. When the other animals saw the lion approaching, they were terrified and ran away. The lion was astonished. "It's true. Every animal is afraid of this rabbit."

The lion turned around and ran away.

See? That's what happens. That's what happens when you do not know who you are. In this life, in this existence is the greatest gift you will ever receive.

The other day I was watching a documentary shot in Egypt about finding a mummy. The anthropologists and professors and doctors were asking, "Who was he? We have to find out who he was."

He was as you will be. If somebody found you in three thousand years' time, they would say, "There was somebody there. Who was it?"

You're probably not an anthropologist. I am not a professor. Yet I am asking the same question: "Who are you?" Ask that question while you're still alive because the answer is profound. Socrates said the same thing: "Know thyself!" Amazing things happen when you put the spotlight on the self.

Do you know who you are? You are the custodian of
the holiest thing in existence. You're the custodian of
this incredible miracle that is the breath that is coming
into you. You're the custodian of this most beautiful
of things called "knowing." You are the custodian of
this most profound power to be kind, of this profound
power called "joy," this profound power called "clarity."

Human beings are so attracted to distractions. This is
a bad habit that robs you of the essential things that
you need to make this life a beautiful occasion. Do you
realize what the difference is between a magician and a
pickpocket? The magician gives you back your wallet.

The fundamentals of being a magician and a pickpocket
are distraction. They both have to distract you.

A pickpocket will take a five-dollar bill and throw it
to the ground while you are waiting there with your
luggage. His accomplice will come by and say, "Excuse
me, I think you dropped a five-dollar bill." You reach to
pick it up and your luggage is gone. Distraction.

Do not be distracted. Focus.

What will you lose if you don't focus? What will the
pickpocket steal from you? When you do not focus, the
understanding of every breath that is coming inside
of you is lost. This is what is stolen. You no longer
recognize the very thing that is bringing you the gift of
life. You no longer recognize existence. You no longer
recognize the passion of the heart. You no longer
recognize your own thirst. You no longer recognize your
calling to be fulfilled. Sleight of hand and it is gone.

We know how incredible it is to be alive, but we allow ourselves to be overwhelmed by incredibly trivial things. A leaf blowing in the wind has more force than some of the things that we allow ourselves to be distracted by.

This is the condition of this world. Unconsciousness prevails. And through this whole drama that is taking place, a breath just came, a miracle just came, and went and came.

Open yourself to understanding yourself, what lies in you. To have in this life not fear, not confusion, but gratitude. To have in this life not questions, but answers. To have in this life not ugliness, but beauty. To have in this life not the barren desert, but a green field that yields the crop of contentment every single day.

Having the knowledge of all things in this world is fine. But if you don't know who you are, it is incomplete. Do you know who you are? You are, in this moment that you are alive, the recipient of the most beautiful, most abundant, and most divine gift of all. Because you are alive, you are the recipient of this breath.

Without this breath, you neither have a personality nor a life. This breath is your candle. In this darkness, it is your candle.

4   Acceptance

Accept that simplicity. Accept that joy in your life. Every day take a step closer to this heart. Every day take a step closer to this existence. Every day become a true disciple of this breath.

When this breath comes into you—and it just did—nobody can say, "I have been breathing for sixty years, so it's okay if I don't breathe for six hours." No, it's not okay. Each breath is needed. Every day, joy and peace need to be accepted, felt, understood.

Be an apprentice. Learn something from life every single day, because life is giving you the opportunity to learn. The value of each breath is being taught. The value of this existence is being taught.

Unopened Letters

There is a story about a man who used to dream of all the things he wanted in his life. He would dream of marrying a beautiful girl, having a position in the government, a nice-paying job, and some land.

So, he was very good at dreaming, but he had no sense of reality. In fact, he would not pay any attention to what was going on around him. He even ignored letters sent to him, and left them unopened.

One day he got old, and he looked at his life. He thought about his dreams, lamenting that none of them had become a reality. He sat down in his living room, and suddenly became aware of the huge pile of letters that had accumulated over the years. So he started opening them.

To his amazement, there was a letter written a long time ago from his girlfriend who wanted to marry him. He called her, and she said, "I waited for you, but I got no answer, so I went ahead and married someone else."

He opened another letter and it was from the king, giving him an appointment to a great job. He called the palace, and the king said, "I waited and waited for you, but you never responded. So the job was given to someone else."

As he opened each letter, he realized that all his dreams had come true, but he wasn't there to accept them. If only he had seen the reality, he wouldn't be lamenting. He could be celebrating.

What happened in this story also happens with us. We have our dreams, our hopes, and our aspirations, and at the base of every hope and dream we have lies the wish to be fulfilled, the wish to be happy, the wish to be content.

The letter that comes to us every day is in the form of this breath. But we don't open it because we're too busy dreaming, trying to come up with formulas and ideas of how we can be content. But happiness itself is included in each one of these envelopes of breath that we are gifted. Only when it is too late do we look at these and start to open them. Only then do we say how precious they are, and look at all the ones we have wasted.

It is so important that in this time we have, we acknowledge what we have been given, that we acknowledge the reality of existence, which is so beautiful, so real, so simple, and which is such a blessing.

Marvel every day at the power that makes the sun rise,
that gives light to the moon.

We get caught in our ideas of how it should be.

The one you truly are in love with is inside of you, and by its very nature cannot leave you until the end of your life. By its very nature, the breath that is coming to you every moment is inseparable from you.

Fall in love with it because it is beautiful. Accept this breath. The day you do, that will be the most incredible act of worship you will ever have done.

Awakening: a transition from sleeping to being awake, from rejection to acceptance, from ignoring every breath to accepting every breath.

Do you have time for this breath?

"Do not disturb. I am busy recognizing the gift of my breath. I am busy receiving the gift of existence."

Each breath is a blessing. Be a fisherman. Cast that net within and catch as many of those blessings as you can. Reel them in.

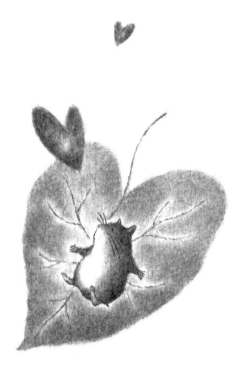

5   Enjoying Life

Enjoy this breath. Who in the whole world will tell you to enjoy your breath? People will tell you to enjoy your meal, enjoy the view, enjoy the movie, enjoy the song, enjoy the flight. Who tells you to enjoy your breath?

If you became comfortable with this existence, with this life, with this moment, with this breath, you would realize a realm of joy unparalleled.

To enjoy each breath one at a time, to understand, to be able to go within: this is the true art of living.

Have you reached a point in your life where you can say, "It is important that I am in touch with this magic of life that is beating, pulsing inside of me. This tide of breath that comes and goes."

Little barnacles sometimes attach themselves to a wall at the edge of the ocean. They cannot move very fast and when the tide goes down, they are exposed and become dry. Then they wait for the tide to come to them again, to bring them sustenance. Their whole existence, every moment, consists of waiting, waiting, waiting for that life to come again.

Do these creatures have a big brain? No. If they have anything, it is just enough for them to get by. But they know when the ocean comes. They know, and they wait.

Their focus is one. Their center is one. Their priority is one. It is to wait for the miraculous water to return, bringing sustenance, bringing the most amazing gift of life. Nobody can make this gift. It is not sold at stores. But it is given, every day. Everywhere this gift of life is being given.

And what do I have? I have eyes that can see. I have ears that can hear. I can feel. I can comprehend. Then why do I not try to comprehend this gift of life? Why do I not try to capture that feeling within me as that miracle shapes my existence? I need to be focused on life like that barnacle.

When that miracle happens, life knows how to celebrate. The little barnacles will open, and they will put out their little fans and they'll dance in the water. Somehow this forceful, thundering, destructive ocean comes and brings a little gift for this tiny little barnacle every day. And it celebrates.

That same power that touches them touches us, too. Do we know how to celebrate when breath comes and goes and comes again?

As a drop of water is to the thirsty, as hope is to the desperate, as the sun is to the sunflower, as nectar is to the bee, as food is to the hungry, let each breath be that for you and me.

One thing that every human being can use, and yet is most deficient in, is appreciation. Doctors won't tell you this. This does not show up on your blood test. They do not do blood tests for appreciation. But we are all deficient in appreciation. We don't know the beauty of the things we have been given. We don't understand the beauty of this breath.

Once you understand the beauty of this breath, how can you not appreciate it? So, appreciate. Enjoy. When you enjoy that feeling, sometimes you will shed tears—not of sorrow, but of joy.

Then you begin to understand the difference between the two. You will experience not the emotion of darkness, but the first rays of that light emanating from the heart.

It's not about pain or suffering. It's the other end of the spectrum—about truly celebrating every breath that comes. Why is it so beautiful? All the logic in the world is not equal to taking it in and enjoying what this heart has to offer. The heart is as much a part of you as is your brain. Give it the equal billing that it needs. Give it the equal time that it needs, and your life will begin to change.

We need to become aware when confusion has set in. Tolerance is not a good alternative. If we allow ourselves to become numb to those things, how will we be able to acknowledge joy in our lives? How will we be able to celebrate the coming and going of this breath?

A human being is, by default, made to experience that joy. There's no upper limit. The dice are loaded. It isn't fair play. The dice are loaded in favor of being fulfilled. To be away from darkness. To be one with this breath. To revel, dance, play with serenity.

It's not a pretend game.

What you get to know is this breath, this moment called now. You get to know fulfillment.

Swing. Swing in the swing of this breath. Become a child again.

One breath and another and another. It's the most important thing in your existence.

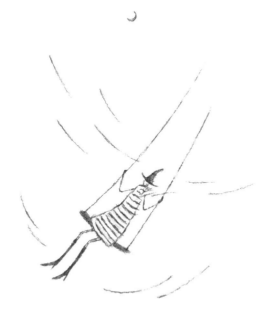

People wonder, "Why does a flower smell or look a particular way?" You may never know. The flower has become a flower for that bee, not for you. You don't have the spectrum of light that a bee can see. It is for that bee that the flower offers its nectar.

You put the little flower up to your nose and say, "How beautiful! Hmm. Smells good." But that little bee looks at the flower and goes, "Hmm. Here I come. You have sweet nectar for me? Give it to me." And it flies with its tiny little wings and finds the flower and the nectar.

You've got a bigger nose, you've got GPS, you've got cellular phones, and you've got 747s, but when it comes to collecting that little bitty nectar from that flower, the bee has you defeated in technology.

Once the bee has made the honey, you can carry it in your 747s and Gulfstreams and Learjets and Citations. But the bee has the technology to find the nectar and enjoy it.

You also have to become a bee and start looking for the flower of life. In every breath, there is a flower, and in every flower, there is a little nectar. Stretch your wings and find that flower and nectar in every breath, and be fulfilled. Fill your cup with that incredible sweet honey gathered from the flowers of the breath.

I will sit down and welcome my breath. I will go within and feel the peace in my heart. I will feel the joy and allow it to come into my life. I will acknowledge my simplicity. I will acknowledge my breath and with open arms embrace the joy and beauty that dwell within me.

To be addicted to joy in your life: this is who you are. People take a deep breath and call it a sigh. For someone who understands the meaning of that breath, another day is welcomed; another moment is welcomed. How beautiful that is. How precious that is. Because what we're shooting for is a very noble cause: to be fulfilled.

We know how to celebrate birthdays. We know how to celebrate weddings. We even know how to celebrate the opening of buildings. But we don't know how to celebrate being us. There will be times that will be difficult, and there will be times that will be easy. But don't forget to celebrate your existence.

6 A Thankful Heart

Every day that we can be thankful for this gift of life is
a day that has been worth living. The cycle is complete.
The sun did not rise in vain. The sun did not set in vain.
The breath that came did not go in vain. The rotating
of this earth, the movement of all the universe was not
in vain.

What do most people feel every single day? They feel
confusion. What do they ask themselves? "Where is this
going?"

We human beings are the most fortunate. We should
not be asking, "Where is this going?" We should be
saying, "Thank you for where it is going. Thank you
for this breath. Thank you for this life. Thank you for
today."

I am in awe of the strength of this existence. I am in awe of the power of this breath. I am in awe of that engine that moves, shapes, pushes, molds, and evolves.

I too have that same life, that existence. And in my life I need to do everything possible to pay the most magnificent tribute to this existence, to this breath, every single day of my life.

When I am me, I'm the happiest. That doesn't mean when I'm alone. It has nothing to do with being alone. When I am me, who I am, who breathes and feels gratitude in their heart for being alive, this is me. A thankfulness that I am alive.

Thank you for this life. Thank you for this breath. Thank you for this existence.

People ask, "Well, who am I thanking?" What difference does it make? Whoever you need to thank will receive the thanks.

You cannot explain breath. You need to breathe it. It cannot be explained. It can only be felt. If you begin to understand that, then a whole different door opens up to you. Not through explanations, but by feeling the preciousness and the joy of this life. The truest responsibility is to be in gratitude to that most magnificent power that has made it possible for you to be alive.

In its purest and most potent form, my gratitude for this life is for the gift itself: not what it enables me to do, but just the experience of existing in this world, right now.

When you learn to express gratitude, you will know what living is all about.

This is how gratitude can be, not just for a moment, but flowing all the time. And what I am thankful for is this breath. To be alive! If you aren't thankful for that, it doesn't matter what else you're thankful for. Because without this breath, without this life, without this existence, there is nothing.

The power of this breath comes into you, even though you are surrounded by all those things that would steal it. There is a wisdom inside you that defies all ignorance. The light inside you defies the darkness all around you. There is a well inside you that defies the drought all around you. The day you discover that wisdom, the day you discover that light, the day you discover that beauty, you will be filled with gratitude. In that perfect moment of gratitude, all distractions fade away.

Even in your last breath, you should be thankful for this life. That's a good goal to have. That's like thanking the host. "Hey, that was good. A grand ride, a great ride. It was a wonderful time."

Those are the fortunate ones who can in their life accept the blessings that they have been given. Humbly to be able to say, "Yes, Yes, I breathe. I'm thankful for every breath, every single breath that comes in and out of me."

Gratitude isn't something we think into being—it's something we *feel*. This song of gratitude plays for me when I take the journey from the outside to the inside.

The greatest form of prayer is to express gratitude.

III.

Peace Through Breath

1 An Abandoned Field

Peace is a fundamental need. Peace is not a luxury. Peace is not a word. Peace is a feeling.

Like we need to sleep, like we need to eat, like we need to drink water, like we need to breathe air, we need peace in our lives.

Without that peace, our functioning breaks down, our basic thinking breaks down, our perceptions break down, we can no longer function as a human being. This is why peace is important.

Peace is already there inside every person. It is just a matter of nurturing what is good.

What is the difference between a garden and an abandoned field? One has been nurtured. Roses have been planted. Grass has been watered. Beautiful flowers will grow. In the abandoned field things are also growing. But they are weeds and there is rubbish everywhere.

The world is in turmoil and pain because the field has been abandoned.

Success and suffering may run through our lives, but peace is constant.

Heaven and Hell

There once was a king, and he had to attack his neighboring kingdom. So, all night long he kept thinking, "I might die! I might get killed. Will I be going to heaven, will I be going to hell? Will I be going to heaven, will I be going to hell?" All night long this kept bothering him, "Will I be going to heaven or hell, heaven or hell, heaven or hell?"

Next day he put on his armor and he got on his horse. He marched out with a big army following him. But he was still being bothered by the thought, "Will I go to heaven? What is heaven? What is hell? What is heaven? What is hell?" It was bothering him, really bothering him.

Then he saw a wise man approaching from the
other direction. He trotted over to the wise man,
got down from the horse, and said, "I have a
question for you. What is heaven? And what is
hell?"

The wise man replied, "Sorry, I don't have the
time. I'm on my way. I'm late."

This made the king furious. "Do you know who
I am? I am the king! And I asked you a simple
question: 'What is heaven, what is hell?' And you
couldn't answer me! What's wrong with you!?"
The king's rage grew and grew. He got angrier
and angrier.

The wise man said, "King, now you are in hell."

The king was shocked! But immediately he realized, "Oh my God. This guy is really wise! What have I done? I mean, I was yelling at him." The king said, "I'm so sorry! I didn't realize! You're absolutely right! That was so wise, so wonderful. I'm very thankful to you for pointing that out to me! Thank you, thank you! I'm clear. I understand! That truly was hell."

And the wise man said, "King, now you are in heaven."

So, are you in heaven? Because if you're not, that's where you belong. Hell isn't good for you.

You need to feel hope every single day. You need to feel heaven every single day. You need to feel peace every single day. Once is not sufficient.

Can you live by just eating once in your life? No. Do you need to drink water every day? Yes! Do you need to sleep every night? Yes! And in the same way, you need to be in peace every single day.

The inspiration to be in peace comes when you listen to your heart. We don't hear the wish of this heart to be content. To have joy. To feel gratitude every single day. To be inspired by the magic of all magics—the most miraculous, the coming and going of this breath.

We have forgotten what it is like to be alive. Instead of celebrating our existence, we are ready to kill each other. That's shameful! Regardless of the reason.

People say, "There are so many hungry people in this world." Why do you think they're hungry? Because they were made like that? No. They're hungry because of human greed. You think enough food is not produced? Half of the total food production of this earth is wasted every year. People could be fed easily.

Poverty? Who made poverty? People made poverty. It's greed: "My-my-my-my-mine!"

In the face of all that is horrible, there is hope. If we humans can dip so low, then we can also climb so high as to make the difference.

The King's Desserts

The king summoned his chef. "Today," he said, "I want you to make the most delicious dessert for me." The chef nodded and went back to the kitchen. This may not seem an unreasonable request, but it is what happened every day. The king wanted the most delicious dessert every night. And the routine was starting to wear thin for the chef.

Every evening the king had his dinner, and no matter what the chef conjured up, the king was not satisfied. "The most delicious dessert" is all the chef heard, night after night. Well, today he was going to do something about it and give the king something to remember. And remember it the king did!

After dinner, the most sumptuous dessert was brought in front of the king. The aroma filled the palace. Everyone who smelled it felt their mouths beginning to water. Tonight the chef had outdone himself.

As the king began to feast on the dessert, he noticed that mice from all around the palace had been drawn into the royal dining room by the wonderful smell. They were everywhere. The dining table began to fill up with mice. They were crawling on the curtains and not even the king's beard was spared as the mice searched for any tiny morsel of the leftover dessert.

This was a royal disaster. Mice everywhere—on the carpet, over the paintings and tapestries—and more were still coming.

An emergency meeting had to be convened to ascertain how to deal with the problem. Clearing his throat, the king said, "What will we do? We have been invaded by mice. Speak up if anyone has any ideas."

The ministers talked among themselves and declared, "Your Royal Highness, we have come to the conclusion that cats should be called in to clear the mice." This seemed reasonable. The general was summoned and given orders that all the cats in the kingdom were to be collected and brought to the palace immediately.

Soon the cats started to appear and this did indeed get rid of the mice, but now the palace was full of cats. Cats, cats, everywhere! Scratching everything, lounging on the royal furniture, sharpening their claws on the royal curtains. The constant meows and purrs were almost deafening.

It was time for another meeting. The king started off, "Well, any more ideas?"

As before, the ministers got into a loud argument. After some time they declared, "Your Royal Highness, we recommend you bring in dogs, because cats don't like dogs." The general was summoned and ordered to round up all the dogs in the kingdom and bring them to the palace.

Soon the cats were replaced by dogs. Now there was nothing but barking, and the dogs were a little less discreet with their personal habits.

It was time for another meeting and this time it was decided that as dogs were afraid of tigers, the kingdom's tigers should be rounded up and brought to the palace. Soon the dogs started to disappear and the palace began to fill up with tigers. This posed a serious problem! The tigers were not only ferocious, but no one dared move a muscle, afraid that the tigers might attack them.

With great difficulty, another meeting was convened and it was decided that elephants be immediately summoned to the palace, because tigers were afraid of elephants.

No sooner had the elephants started to arrive than the tigers fled, leaving things in a bigger mess than before.

Now the whole palace was full of elephants and there was no place to move. The elephants were breaking things and the disaster was absolutely intolerable. Pretty soon the palace started to fill up with elephant dung. The stench was indescribable.

Well, it was time for another meeting and this time it was decided that mice should be called in, because elephants were afraid of mice. The general complied and as the mice started to arrive, the elephants left. Everyone at the palace found themselves back where they started, with mice everywhere.

The king now realized that he was actually to blame for the whole fiasco. Had it not been for his greed this never would have happened.

Problems are created by us, and the solutions also reside with us. Discover your being, your self, because in that self there is everything that you need. Learn the language of the heart and feel what you have been missing.

Conflict doesn't just happen across borders. Conflict can happen inside a country. Conflict can happen inside a town. Conflict can happen inside a house. Conflict can happen inside ourselves.

War begins in the minds of human beings. Conflict does not begin on the outside. Conflict begins on the inside, and the resolution of the conflict is also on the inside.

Do you know what it is like to stop in the middle of your war and feel the peace that dances within you?

Inner peace gives you a rock-solid and unchangeable foundation at the heart of your being.

A few years back a photographer decided to do an experiment. He took a huge stainless steel mirror and placed it in the jungle. Monkeys are the most curious, so they came and stood in front of the mirror. They started screaming, showing their teeth, hitting the mirror, freaking out, and running away.

Then a big gorilla turned up. He stood in front of the mirror and screamed. He beat his chest to say, "Who are you?" He was extremely angry. He screamed and beat his chest again. He paced back and forth and back and forth and back and forth. Why? Do you know why? He did not recognize himself. That gorilla he was seeing was not an enemy. It was him. The gorilla was becoming his own worst enemy.

Are we seeing ourselves in the mirror and not recognizing ourselves? When we kill each other, we kill ourselves. When we rob from each other, we rob from ourselves.

Because you and you and you and you are my reflection. You and you and you and you are each other's reflection in that mirror. When you become angry at each other, you are only angry at yourself. When you tell a lie, you tell a lie to yourself. When you harm each other, you only harm yourself. Because you do not recognize it is you.

Someone lives in Taiwan, someone lives in Japan, someone lives in India, someone lives in Canada, someone lives in America, someone lives in Mexico, someone lives in Argentina, someone lives in Brazil, someone lives in England. Do you think there would be differences? They speak different languages, they eat different kinds of food, some of them even drive on the wrong side of the road!

But they all experience joy, they all experience pain, they all experience hope, they all experience disappointment. Everywhere in the world we experience the same thing. Maybe we use different words, but they are the same thing.

Peace is inside everyone and always will be. The question becomes, "Why don't you feel it?" The reason we don't feel that peace is because so much that is not real comes between us and that peace. People come from other countries, and you say, "Oh that person must be different." We have learned how to make buildings. We have learned how to make airplanes. We have learned how to make cars. We have learned how to make this and that. We have even learned how to make wars. And we have learned how to make the instruments for the wars. But we have not learned how to be in peace.

People fight in the name of religion. Where they should be respecting life, they look at life as something trivial. What happened that we got to this point where the basic respect for one another is gone? To see somebody, whether they are a Muslim or a Hindu or a Christian, and say, "Enjoy your connection, enjoy what you believe in." What happened? All of a sudden it becomes, "No, you are inferior, I am superior."

How long will this go on? I am a voice for peace. Just a small voice. But when my voice joins with all the other people who want peace, it becomes a very loud voice.

Confusion, madness, desperation, greed! It's unbelievable how much greed there is in this world.

I wish the greed was there for peace. I wish the greed was there to help each other.

But, no, the greed is there just to fill your own pocket, somehow, and that's all that matters. Greed, anger, fear.

People say, "World peace is not possible because there's so much greed." I was thinking about that. "Greed, greed. There's a lot of greed in this world." Then I thought, "Well there must be an antidote to greed." And I found it. It's called appreciation.

Greedy people can never appreciate. They can't! But as soon as they start appreciating, you know what happens?

You, the human, kicks in. And you know what your nature is? When you likc something—there's a song playing on the radio that you like—you turn up the volume. You want to share it!

You want to share. You're cooking something in the kitchen and it's good. What happens? "Taste this. Taste this." You are putting on a dress and you look beautiful. What do you want to do? Show it.

Even with all the greed in the world, appreciation still exists. And appreciation kills greed.

But people don't appreciate because they're only on one track: "More. More. More. More. More. More." If they start appreciating it—if they actually start enjoying what they have—they'll say, "Wow, this is good! Let me share this!" Because that's human nature. And you are a human being.

If absence of war is peace, then why is it that wars start again after the wars are over? Because that is just political peace. Political peace is not the peace that resides within you. War is a symptom, not the disease. When people are in peace, wars could end—if that's what they decided. Because the real war begins with you.

A long time ago, it was the king who had to go in front of the battle. Negotiations were of utmost importance, because nobody wanted to get killed. Today, the same kings sit behind lofty palaces and send other people to do their dirty work.

If you really need to have a war, have some company create a video game and the two leaders can play it. Whoever wins, wins! And that would be good enough.

Who gets killed when wars happen? The innocent get killed when wars take place. It is not the perpetrators, it is the innocent people who get killed. It is the children who suffer. It is these children who will never see their dad, who will never know their father. They will grow up with hatred in their heart, where there should be peace, where there should be enjoyment, where there should be love—they will have hatred towards that country that killed their father. How sad is that?

Peace is not just an idea. It is a necessity.

How precious are you? Unfathomable! So long as the divine is in you, it's unfathomable. When the divine is gone? Nothing. You do not know how to respect yourself. Something is wrong. You are only looking at the outer case, not what's in it. The day you have a recognition of what is in it will be the day when the idea of peace will begin to make sense.

If what's taking place in the world today keeps
happening, the human race is not going to be around
for long. It is self-destroying! Why does a person kill
another person? Because they don't even know the
person they're about to kill. They're standing far away;
they have a gun. They point the gun, look through the
little scope, and say, "I got one!" Pow! And the person is
dead. And someone can push a button to kill hundreds
of thousands of people in a country they have never
visited.

My commitment is to peace. In my travels around
the world, I've experienced a lot of things, the most
baffling of which is people's explanation of why there
can't be peace. People focus on the symptoms, but not
the disease. My efforts are focused on eliminating the
disease: people not being in touch with themselves, not
knowing who they are.

If we don't take care of the disease, the symptoms will never go away. And we all know what the symptoms look like: greed, war, selfishness, violence, and an increasing loss of trust. Peace is a real thing. Peace resides in the heart of every human being. Peace has to emanate from each of us.

When you can experience that joy in your life, when you can understand the value of this breath, then you have truly begun to understand what life is.

This world needs to understand what life is all about.
So much energy is spent just to destroy, so little to bring
peace to people.

Peace is about heaven on earth. Peace is about good times. Peace is about enjoying life. Peace is about construction, not destruction.

It is time to practice peace. It is time to practice consciousness. It is time to practice kindness. It is time to practice embracing each other. It is time not to pretend to be intelligent, but to be intelligent. It is time not to pretend to like peace, but to like peace. It is time not to pretend to have peace, but to have peace.

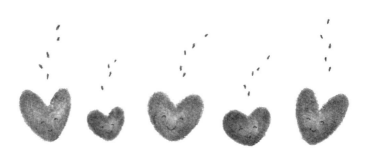

2   One Step at a Time

If we practice greed, then that is what we will get good
at. If we practice peace, then that is what we will get
good at. If we practice anger, then that is what we
will get good at. If we practice tolerance, then that is
what we will get good at. If we practice looking at each
other with compassion, then that is what we will get
good at. What are you practicing?

If human beings can start wars, they surely can make
peace. There is no "they" that will bring peace to us.
Peace is not going to come in a package or a box. Peace
is not going to come as rain from the heavens.

The possibility of peace has already been given to every human being on earth. We have to discover the need for peace within. And then create an environment where people can be free to feel that peace in their lives.

It begins with each one of us. A journey of a thousand miles begins with the first step. It will happen one step at a time, and that one step begins with you. If you can take that first step in your life, you can complete the journey of a thousand miles. And yes, peace is possible.

Do we live in a society where peace is a priority? Or do we live in a society where justifications for war are sought? Which one? We don't live in a society where every day the mission of every citizen is to be kind. No.

We see somebody taking our parking spot and a war could start.

People say there is so much greed in this world there will never be peace. People say there is so much anger in this world there will never be peace. But they have not understood what our nature is.

Two Wolves

Once there was a settlement in a beautiful valley. One day a little boy approached the chief and said, "I have a question."

The chief asked, "What is it?"

The boy said, "Chief, I see some people are good sometimes and the same people are bad sometimes. How can that be? If somebody is good they should always be good. How can this be?"

The chief replied, "Inside of you there are two wolves. There is a good wolf and a bad wolf, and they fight."

The boy thought about it and then said, "Chief, why do they fight?"

The chief said, "To gain supremacy over you."

The boy thought more and then asked, "Chief, which wolf wins—the good wolf or the bad wolf?"

And the chief answered, "The wolf you feed."

You want peace in your life? Begin with this. If you find yourself getting upset, take a tiny second to reflect: "Good wolf, bad wolf? Oops, I am feeding the bad wolf. When I feed the bad wolf, I am rewarded with anger, fear, confusion, and pain. When I feed the good wolf, I am rewarded with clarity and understanding, and my heart dances." Feed the good wolf! It is simple and it works. If we can understand our nature, who we really are, maybe we can make a difference in our lives.

If that peace is everywhere, then why don't I feel it? It is closer to me than my shadow. Why don't we see it?

Because we haven't got the eyes to see it. What kind of eyes do you need? You need the pure eyes of a child.

To see, not through judgment, but from discovery, from feeling. Not from ideas, but from feeling.

Once you understand the importance of today, you can start to understand now, because that is where you live.

By the rules of time, you are not allowed to live in tomorrow. You are not allowed to live in yesterday. You can only exist in now.

Welcome in your life this moment of existence, because that is the address of peace. Now is where peace resides.

People think you have to renounce everything to find peace.

Who started this incredible lie? People say, "I am a family man. I cannot give up everything. I have a house, I have children, I have responsibilities, so I cannot have peace, sorry."

You don't need to give up everything. When the peace is inside of you, what happens on the outside makes no difference.

Where is the peace that we are looking for? Inside of us. Where do people say it is? On top of a mountain.

Do you think the top of the mountain has peace? No. When storms come, it gets very wild. But we don't look where peace is. Inside of us.

A moment of positive choosing can be the start of a life-changing journey to inner calm, focus, contentment, and peace.

We forget the power of this breath. So we prepare to search. We plan to read a book or visit a particular place. But there is something happening right here: your breath.

People are crying out for peace. Peace is not a luxury. Peace is as important as breathing air, eating food, and having shelter, because it is the fundamental necessity of every heart on the face of this earth.

Peace is not a new concept. As long as there have been wars (in the history of mankind), there has been a voice that has called out again and again for peace—true peace, real peace—a peace that is experienced by every individual.

Peace is something that comes from the heart of human beings, not from the mind.

What happens when a person is in peace? There is a recognition. There is a simplicity. There is an appreciation. There is a gratitude. This is what happens: recognition of each other, recognition that my need is like yours. That isn't about power. That isn't about destruction. But it is about preserving that which is precious. It is about appreciating the gift that we have been given. It is about being alive.

I have been speaking in public since I was four years old, talking about peace. My effort has been to look at a person and just see a human being, not a woman, not a man, not poor, not rich, not Indian, not African. When I look at somebody, I just want to see a human being.

The world has told me, "No, you must know he's a Christian, he's a Muslim, she's a Hindu, he's an American, they're Nepalese, she's Sri Lankan, he's from Africa, he's from Canada." All my life I have not found one single good thing that came from seeing somebody as a Christian, or a Muslim, or a Hindu, as a woman, as a man, as a rich person, as poor. It does nothing! Nothing!

When I look at people, I feel love for them because they are human beings. Who am I to judge, if the breath is not judging? The breath is coming into them. The breath is coming into me.

Everyone has a reason for why peace can't happen. Some people have two or three, or four or five, or maybe a hundred.

Do you know how many reasons I have for why there should be peace? I have eight billion reasons for why there should be peace, because that is how many people live on the face of this earth.

Something inside of us says, "You need peace in your life." Now, you can call it many things. That's just semantics. You can call it "peace." You can call it "happiness." You can call it "joy." You can call it "bliss." It doesn't matter. But that peace is inside each one of us.

As human beings, we have a need—not a need created by society, but a fundamental need to be fulfilled, to be in peace. It is easy to toss around the word "peace." But what is peace? Is it just hearing wind chimes? No traffic? No airplanes or trains buzzing by?

Or is peace a feeling? An undeniable feeling not born of thought. Everything that comes to us is born of thought. We get good news and we think, "Things are going my way." We get bad news and we think, "Why is this happening to me?"

Peace is that place, not full of definitions, but full of feeling.

It doesn't take much for us to get unsettled. It happens when we're in traffic and somebody honks their horn. Your son or daughter tells you, "I failed," and you get upset. So is peace simply not being upset?

What is peace? What does it mean to be here, to be alive?

Breath—the coming and going of this breath. Out of nowhere it comes and to nowhere it goes. From this breath comes the gift of life. You can be. You can admire. You can be thankful that you exist. You can feel and give kindness. You can know that all is well.

Peace is inside of you, so why do you look for it on the outside? Are you really looking for peace or are you looking for fulfillment of an idea. Do you want real peace in your life?

Or do you just want to repeat, "I'm in peace. I'm in peace. I'm in peace. I am in peace." Which do you want—the peace that dances in your heart or a badge that says, "I am in peace"? If you want a badge or a T-shirt or a tattoo saying "I am in peace," I can't help. I don't have them. Which peace do you want?

Everybody has a vision of utopia. Whether it is in our home life, in our business, or in the world, whenever peace is talked about, the idea of utopia crops up. But the word "utopia" derives from two Greek words meaning "not" and "place." So what the word actually means is "nowhere." It does not exist anywhere! The only place you can truly have this utopia is within you. Not out there. Within you. And breath is calling you every day to experience this utopia.

What is peace? Is peace some idea? Utopia? Everybody will be dancing. Everybody will have flowers in their hair. Nobody will argue. No problems in the parking lot.

That's not peace.

Peace is all that is good in you. Peace is the serenity in you. Peace is the kindness in you. Peace is the gentleness in you. Peace is the understanding in you. Peace is the appreciation in you. Peace is the light in your heart. Peace is the joy in you. Peace is the divine in you. Peace is the acceptance of the blessing in you. Peace is the coming and going of the breath in you. Peace is the beauty that you are.

Telling you about tomorrow is a guessing game. But let me tell you what is happening in this moment: the breath has come into you, it's going, and it's coming, and you're alive.

Because you're alive, of all the feelings that you can feel, there is one that is supreme. And that is called joy.

Of all the states that you can be in, there is one that is supreme and that is the state of clarity.

Of all the possibilities that you can have in this moment, there is one that is supreme and that is contentment, peace.

You have this immense possibility of feeling and embracing life, of understanding the value of each breath that you take.

Immediately, people say: "If I am busy acknowledging the value of my breath, I will have time for nothing else!" Do you say that because you have experienced it?

Or is it some voice that comes into your head, "Nah—it can't be done. Peace? Impossible!"

Where did that come from? Was that written on the sky somewhere? Was it all etched on an apple that you ate? Who said it?

You have forgotten that which is so amazing: that you come here, on this earth, not alone but with peace. That you come with hope, with understanding, with wisdom.

But these are things we don't discuss. Instead we repeatedly discuss our problems. What about the solution? The solution, beautifully, lies inside of you. You have in you what you are looking for. If you can understand that, your life will change.

People ask, "How do I get to peace?" You get to peace like you got to everything else—by having a passion for it.

Start falling in love with peace. Make that peace a priority in your life and you'll find it.

The good news is, it's possible. The good news is, it's within you. The hard part: Do you have the passion? That's the hard part. That's the hard part. Fall in love with life.

And to fall in love with life is the most noble thing a human being can do.

3   Humanity's Finest Achievement

It is not the world that needs peace; it is people. When people in the world are at peace within, the world will be at peace.

People are waiting for some angel to come and to fix their problems. I say to people, "The angel has come." Did you know the angel has come? Do you know who the angel is? You! You are the angel that can change your life.

A lot of people say, "Oh, this will never happen. There's too much greed." I have something to say to you. You know man's mission to the moon? You know why it happened? It was not because of the people who said it couldn't happen. It was because of the people

who said it could happen. That's why it happened.
When you are in love with your life, with your existence,
that's when you begin to respect other people's
existence. This is not the case in the world today. This
needs to change. And that fundamental change doesn't
begin with the world out there. It begins with every
single human being on the face of this earth.

It is not governments, not big institutions, not the
police, not the army, but each human being taking
responsibility for this peace that is going to make a
difference.

The ocean of peace resides inside of you. Not the
canal, not the lake, not the bathtub. Why do we not feel
that peace? Because we do not know ourselves.

Since we've been traveling on this road of life, we've gone in circles, arriving at the same intersection again and again. We need a map. You know what the name of the map is? "Know thyself." The map is a little piece of paper that says, "You are here and you want to go there."

The self is the knowable union of the infinite and the finite. Knowing the self puts us in the driver's seat in life.

Having peace on earth is not difficult. What is difficult is for people to recognize who they are. Because once they recognize that, peace would be automatic. It would not be an issue. The issue is to know who you are.

A breath comes in and a breath goes out and you find yourself alive. The palette of what you can feel, what you can express, what you can know, what you can understand, who you can be, is virtually infinite. There is no limit. This is the realm of the heart. This is the realm of knowing. This is the realm of those people who have understood their dignity and have no problem offering dignity to others.

That's the day this world's going to change. Not because you speak this language and I speak this language, therefore we are friends. But because you are alive and I am alive and therefore we are friends.

If you want peace in your life, know that peace is not far from you, never has been, as it dances in the heart of every single human being.

There's a world waiting. One that you create and become a part of. A world that respects you. A world that understands you. A world that doesn't put labels on everything. A world that welcomes generations of human beings like you as long as this earth exists. When you live full of gratitude, kindness, peace, and joy, you want to stay that way for the rest of your life.

Every year governments fail. Why do they fail? People don't take responsibility. They hand the responsibility to one person: "You take care of it!"

The time has come to change that. The time has come when every citizen of this planet earth needs to take responsibility for the benefit of all mankind and mammal-kind and bird-kind and worm-kind and insect-kind and every kind.

It hasn't worked to keep putting it on somebody else's head, but we keep doing it. What about our responsibilities? What is your responsibility? Your responsibility is to be human. What does it mean to be human? A person who finds peace beautiful.

Peace is going to be mankind's finest achievement. Not rockets, not technology, but peace. All of us have a part to play in making that possible.

What is the birthplace of war, of turmoil? In us. Oh, so peace is inside of us, and turmoil is inside of us? Yes. Darkness is inside of us and light is inside of us.

The curious thing is that the world has found the darkness. The world has found the conflict. The world has found the greed. The world has found the unconsciousness.

But if you can discover anger inside of you, if you can discover doubt inside of you, then you are completely capable of also experiencing the clarity inside you. If we are capable of starting wars, then we are also quite capable of bringing care, respect, understanding, and peace into this world. Because it is just the other side of the coin.

Ignorance and knowledge are neighbors! Clarity and doubt are neighbors. Life and death are neighbors— right next to each other. Darkness and light are neighbors. How close are they? Take away one, and the other one is instantly there! Doesn't take much.

Hope, joy, clarity, understanding . . . that's on one side. Doubt, fear, misery, ignorance is on the other. Which way do you go?

When I see violence of human beings against human beings, it always shocks me. What went wrong that the value of the life of another human being means nothing? Something went horribly wrong.

At some point we have to make a decision: "No!" We
have to change. Forget about "me" and bring in "us."
All of us. Too much of this "me" mentality exists. Over
time people have switched to "me, me, me, gimme,
gimme, gimme." We have tried the "me" but it didn't
work so well.

The time has come to change the "me" to "us." That
all of us are on this planet earth. That all of us need
to understand what it means to be alive. That all of us
need to help each other. We shouldn't be devising ways
of killing each other—we should be devising ways of
helping each other.

It requires a change in consciousness. Not "me" but "us." And "us" is everyone on this earth. Because that is the only solution that we haven't tried.

Is it possible to turn on the light of peace and dignity in the heart of humanity? Where is the switch? That's the problem. It's not one switch; it's eight billion switches and each one needs to be turned on. Can it be done? Yes.

Peace is not something that needs to be created. Peace is not something that is an end result of a bunch of actions. With all our problems, with all our wars, with all our trouble, there is peace inside of every single human being. It's already there.

Elephant Rope

One day there was a man who had never seen an elephant. He found out about a village where they had huge elephants, and traveled there. Never having seen an elephant before, he was really surprised. But what surprised him even more was that the elephants were tied with just a very thin rope around their feet.

How could such enormous elephants be held in place by such little ropes? He went to the headman and said, "These elephants are strong, aren't they?"

"Yes, very, very strong," the headman replied.

"Then how can such a huge animal, so strong and powerful, be held back with just this tiny little rope?"

The headman explained, "When these were baby elephants, we used to tie them with these little ropes. They tried to move but they couldn't. As they grew, we kept them tied with the same little ropes. Now that they have grown big and strong, they have stopped trying and they think that the tiny rope can still hold them in place. Of course if they tried, the rope would not hold back such a powerful animal. But the elephants have given up trying."

Why did I tell this story? Because in a way this is what is happening. You are much bigger than the sum of your problems. But these problems come. They're holding you back and you do not realize your own power. You don't realize your own strength. That as a human being you have the strength in you to go beyond these barriers.

We the people of this planet earth are responsible for its destiny. We look toward leaders to solve our problems. Our reliance needs to be on us, not on the leaders. Us bringing hope to each other. Us lighting the way for each other.

There is no reason for war. War should not even be an option! Talk it out, settle your differences. To kill another person for a reason, for your reason, cannot be accepted, not in this day and age or ever.

Become simple, and feel the dignity. Become simple, and see what the reality is. It's the same sun that shines over the Arab world, that shines over the Indian world, that shines over the Malaysian world, the Australian world, the American world, the Canadian world, the South American world—everywhere! It's the same sun. We live on the same beautiful planet.

The world teaches us differences. I want to point out the similarities. Because then we can all feel dignified. We can all feel that simplicity. We can all feel each other's burden, feel each other's pain, and participate in each other's passion. That is civilization.

It is on the stage of the heart, in each individual human being, where peace needs to dance. This doesn't require wishes but determination. This doesn't require definitions but clarity. If we can go to the moon, it should certainly be possible to travel the shortest distance there is: from one person to his or her own heart. To feel the joy that exists in all of us.

Know the difference between wisdom and knowledge. Acquire knowledge, but use that knowledge wisely. Having knowledge is great. Practicing that knowledge is wisdom.

So there is a lot of technical knowledge in this world, but without that wisdom we're using it to kill each other. Use it wisely, and it could be there to reverse the effects of global warming. Use it wisely, and it could help the polar bears as they lose their habitat. The ills that human beings have done can be reversed by technology, if used wisely.

What you need to garner is empathy. Not sympathy. Empathy. If anything can stop the wars, it is empathy. People don't empathize anymore. To be able to place yourself in the other person's shoes. That doesn't mean you agree with them. It doesn't mean you disagree with them. Just to be able to see their viewpoint.

We don't see their viewpoint and that's why we fight in the name of God. We fight in the name of religion. We fight in the name of peace. We fight in the name of joy.

We fight in the name of all things that have always been held precious on the face of this earth. They have become the fighting points when they should be the saving points for our society. To empathize not only with each other but to empathize even with those animals who are losing their turf.

I see what's happening in this world and it's not good. It's time we change it. The change can only begin with us. Right now we want the change to begin with other people, not us.

That's because we don't know who we are. We are just like them. Knowing yourself has a lot of value.

Who will benefit? We will benefit. Our future generations will benefit. Their children and grandchildren will benefit. This world can be a place they can proudly call their own. I have a very, very strong feeling. If we really want this, it can be done.

4 Come Home

My strategy is very simple: to be in peace with yourself.
It's just you. Nobody else is involved. You be in peace
with yourself. And how can you be in peace with
yourself? Journey to the self. You must know yourself.

Once you know yourself, you then must gain victory
over the self. Not victory over your neighbor or anyone
else. But victory over the self.

When you are victorious over yourself, then you can be
in peace with yourself. And when you are in peace with
yourself, then you make peace with the world. When
enough people make peace with themselves and the
world, then world peace starts to come into view.

When war happens, the innocent die. In the same way, when you are at war with yourself, the innocent moments of your life are being slaughtered.

Each moment of existence is innocent. As it comes to you, it's totally innocent, like a baby. It just brings you possibility.

You can mold it. You can fold it. You can destroy it. You can create a monster out of it if you wish. Or you can have it as the most tender, gentle time with yourself—listening to that feeling that fills the heart and causes gratitude to emerge.

Peace is possible, but it needs a strategy to win the war. And we are going to have a very specific strategy. We are not just going to go out there ad hoc. Because this enemy that we are talking about has been around for a really, really long time.

Anger. Fear. Hate. Been around for much longer than you have. And many, many people have tried to fight it. And they have not won. My strategy is to not spill a drop of blood. Not one single drop of blood. And to win.

You are the battlefield. You are the enemy. And you have to be the victor. That's why there cannot be a single drop of blood. Because it'll be yours. So no blood. Just win. Win. With this mighty armament of clarity. Do you know how many people have been slain by the enemy called doubt? How afraid are you of doubt?

Knowing yourself is the biggest part of this strategy. Because if you don't know yourself, you will never know how strong you are. You might believe how weak you are.

But you will never know how strong you are. You have to be in shape to fight this war. Especially if you don't want any blood spilled.

Discipline is needed. What kind of discipline? To become the ardent admirer of joy. To become the ardent admirer of beauty. To become the recognizer. The biggest journey in your life is the journey of unchanging. It's the journey back to your self, back to your home.

You changed. How far are you from the heart of a child? How much have you changed way out there, lost in la-la land, battered, bruised, broken? Go back home. Go inside and feel divine joy and beauty. Learn how to recognize what is most auspicious.

Sometimes, you may have walked too far away from home. But your home is still there. If you are alive, then the breath is saying to you, "Go home." When you left your home, you left the sanity of home, too. You need to forgive yourself for that. With that forgiveness you can come back home.

In your home is peace. In your home is wisdom. In your home is clarity. In your home is light. In your home is joy. In your home is fulfillment. But the only one that is not home is you. So come home.

Travelers feel relief when they reach their destination.
It is like when you come home or when you find what
you are looking for. Even when you don't know what
you are looking for, you know instantly when you find it
and you say, "This is it. This is what I was looking for."
You feel a tremendous sense of relief.

The journey to the self is a journey to you. When you
come home, you will see the world in a changed way.
The world isn't going to make peace with you. You have
to make peace with the world.

If you want that joy in your life, rediscover in yourself the heart of a child. When we can once again see with the pure eyes of our heart, then we can appreciate the gift we have been given, the gift of existence. That, yes, it means something that I am alive, I was given the gift of life, I was given the gift of this breath again and again and again.

Go within and feel what is happening inside of you, the coming and going of that breath. Feel that beauty. Feel that energy. Feel that reality.

About the Author

© Timeless Today

From boy prodigy and '70s teenage icon to Global Peace Ambassador and *New York Times* bestselling author, Prem Rawat has brought exceptional clarity, inspiration, and deep life learning to millions.

Prem had his first speech published in his native India at just four years old. Now based in the United States but touring internationally nine months every year, Prem Rawat works with people from all walks of life, showing them how to experience the source of peace within themselves. His global efforts span over one hundred countries, bringing a practical message of hope, happiness, and peace to all, one person at a time.

Prem Rawat is the *New York Times* bestselling author of *Hear Yourself: How to Find Peace in a Noisy World* and the creator of the highly successful Peace Education Program now used in eighty-four countries. Prem is a fixed- and rotor-wing pilot with more than 14,500 hours experience. He is a keen photographer, cook, classic car restorer, a father to four children, and a grandfather of four.